Stories from the Quran
Book 2

Abraham *(Ibrahim)* and the Holy House

&

Jonah *(Yunus)* and the Whale

Written by
Noura Durkee
Illustrated by
Simon Trethewey

Abraham and the Holy House

Abraham had a dream.
God told him, "Take your wife
Hajar and your baby son Ismail.
Go to the desert.
Leave them there."

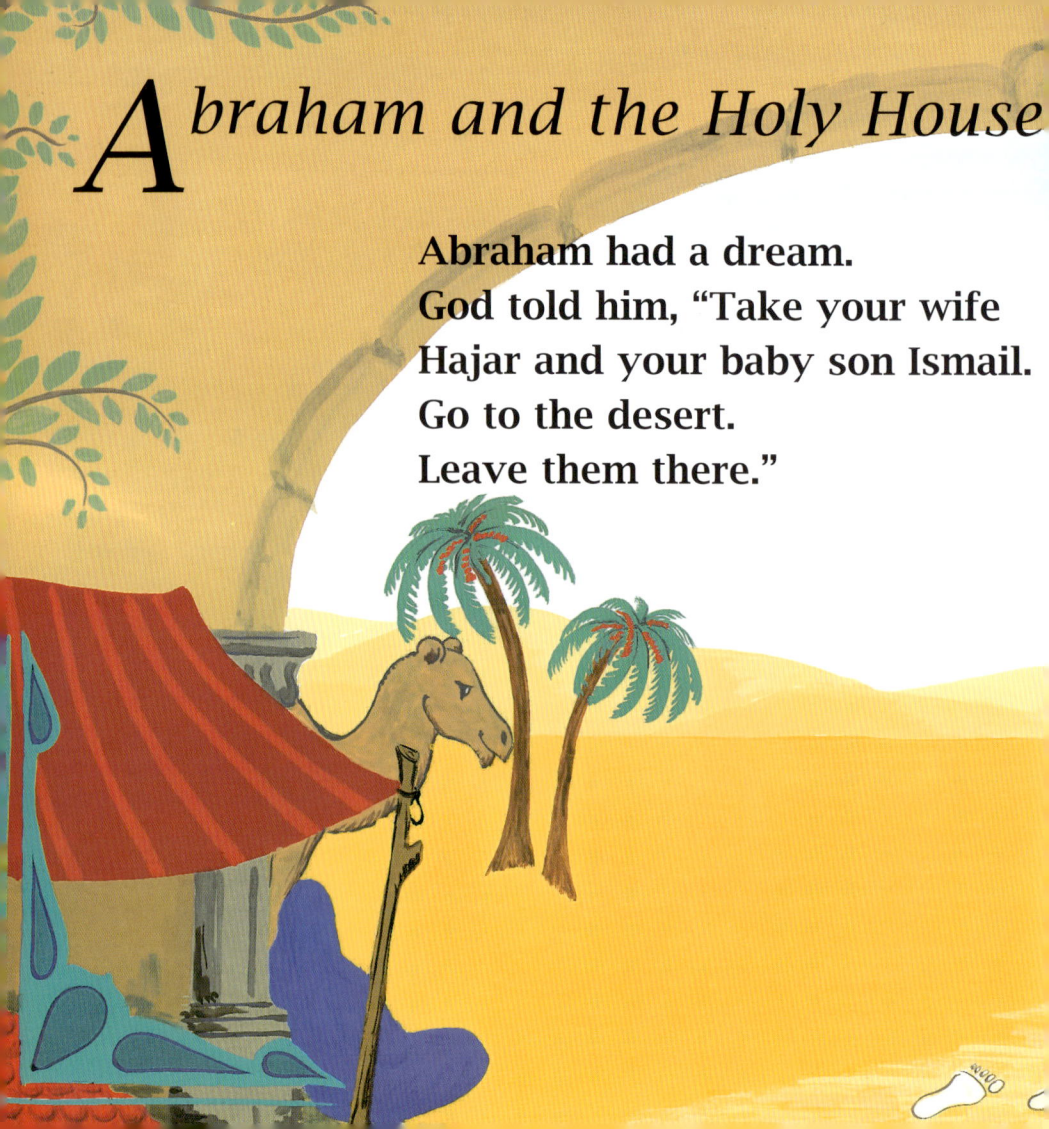

So they took a camel and water and a sack of dates to eat.
Off they went.

It was a long journey.

In the desert, Abraham left as God had told him to do. Ismail ate all the dates.

He drank all the water.
He was still very thirsty.
He cried and cried.

Hajar looked for water.
She ran up and down two hills.
She ran up and down again.

Then *whoosh*, lovely water
bubbled out of the ground!
They called it ZamZam.

Birds came to drink the water.
People came too.
They put up tents and stayed.
Their goats and sheep stayed too.

Soon a town grew there.
Its name was *Mecca*.
Hajar and Ismail lived there.
Abraham often came to visit.

God told Abraham
to build a Holy House in Mecca.
Ismail helped his father.

An angel brought a special black stone.
It was very old.
When the Holy House was built,
they walked around it and prayed.

Abraham asked God to make Mecca a wonderful place.
His prayer was answered.

Years passed....
Many people came to Mecca
from all over the world.
Many people wanted to pray there.

Jonah

and the Whale

Jonah was a Prophet.
He lived in a big city
with lots of people.

Jonah was upset!
He said "They don't care!

They won't listen to me.
I am going to run away.
Far, far away."

Jonah found a ship and got on it.

Soon a huge storm came.
Waves crashed! Winds blew!
The captain said, "God must be angry!"

Jonah began to shake and shiver.
"It's me," he said, "God is angry with me!"

It was dark inside the whale.
Jonah was very scared.
He said to God,
"Nobody can hide from you!
I am very sorry I ran away."

God forgave Jonah and told the whale to take him back home.

The bad people found him.
They were sorry too. They said,

"Teach us to be good."

Copyright © Hood Hood Books 1998
Reprinted 2006

Hood Hood Books
39 Thurloe Street,
London SW7 2LQ

Tel: 44 20 7584 7878
Fax: 44 20 7225 0386
Web-Site: www.hoodhood.com
E-Mail: info@hoodhood.com

British Library Cataloguing–in–Publication Data
A catalogue record for this book is available from the British Library

ISBN 1 900251 51 5

No part of this book may be reproduced
in any form without permission of the publishers.
All rights reserved.

Origination by: *Fine Line Graphics Ltd*, London

PUBLISHER'S NOTE

According to the *hadith* (saying) of the Prophet Muhammad, peace be upon him, it is traditional practice not to depict God's Angels, Messengers and Prophets in any form of visual representation. There are no such depictions in this book.